Shannon Quimby's Color, Create, DECORATE

Creative, Fresh Ideas & Decorating Techniques

emmis

books

For further information, contact the publisher at:

Emmis Books
1700 Madison Road
Cincinnati, Ohio 45206

www.emmisbooks.com

ISBN: 1-57860-207-6
Library of Congress Control Number: 2005931391

Edited by Jessica Yerega
Designed by HUB Collective, Ltd., Portland, Oregon

Acknowledgments

For years this was a common conversation with friends, clients, family, and even strangers:

"You should write a book!"

"Me? Write a book?"

"Yeah! You have all these great decorating ideas, and you need to share them with everyone."

"But I don't know the first thing about how to write a book. Besides, if I write a book, everyone will think I know what I'm doing!"

"Well, Shannon, you do very well at what you don't know how to do!"

So here I am ... with a book under my belt. I am 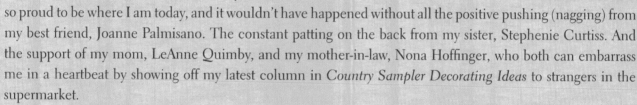 so proud to be where I am today, and it wouldn't have happened without all the positive pushing (nagging) from my best friend, Joanne Palmisano. The constant patting on the back from my sister, Stephenie Curtiss. And the support of my mom, LeAnne Quimby, and my mother-in-law, Nona Hoffinger, who both can embarrass me in a heartbeat by showing off my latest column in *Country Sampler Decorating Ideas* to strangers in the supermarket.

Cindy Cowell and Ann Wilson: The Cowardly Lion in *The Wizard of Oz* found cu-cu-courage, and because of you, I did, too. John O'Neill: Your advice and calm disposition always kept me on track—not an easy task. My photographer, Steve Cridland: We did it! You rock, dude! Susan Sandor: You are an amazing and talented woman. Garth Weber and Lindsey Hammond: This book is beautiful because of the two of you. Emmis Books Editorial Director Jack Heffron: You went all nine rounds for me; thank you. To Jessica Yerega, who came on board and ironed everything out: High five to you!

Special thanks to my three-year-old son, Chase, who is going to grow up to be a football star/baseball star/hoppercopper pilot (that's helicopter, to you and me), for letting me borrow your artistic and inspirational ideas. And to my husband, Glenn Hoffinger, the man who has believed in me from the moment we met: Some day, Handsome, I'll be able to pay for your golf—at least nine holes.

Thanks to the following companies for their generous contributions to the book:

The Back Porch
Owners: Monica Duke and
Lisa Robson
8235 SE 13th Avenue
Portland, OR 97202
503-230-0705
dukemonica@hotmail.com
Antiques, home and garden
accessories

Bernadette Breu Antiques and
Ornaments
1134 NW Everett Street
Portland, OR 97209
503-226-6565
blackpearlwild@hotmail.com
Antiques

Carpet Mill Outlet
9701 SE McLoughlin Boulevard
Milwaukie, OR 97222
503-786-9441
kharrison@corinthian-rugs.com
Rugs

Farmhouse Antiques
Owner: Jean Snook
8028 SE 13th Avenue
Portland, OR 97202
503-232-6757 or 503-253-1762
Antiques

French Quarter
1313 NW Glisan Street
Portland, OR 97209
503-282-8200
www.frenchquarterlinens.com
Home products, bedding and bath

Hippo Hardware
1040 East Burnside Street
Portland, OR 97214
503-231-1444
Antique and reproduction home
products

Hunt & Gather
Owner: Lisa Delaere Breslau
1302 NW Hoyt Street
Portland, OR 97209
503-227-3400
www.huntgather.com
Home products, interior design,
furniture

Lumber Liquidators
800-FLOORING
www.lumberliquidators.com
Wood floors, butcher-block counter tops

Mill End Store
9701 SE McLoughlin Boulevard
Milwaukie, OR 97222
503-786-1234
millendstr@aol.com
www.millendstore.com
Fabrics; provided location shots for this
book

Oblation Paper and Press
516 NW 12th Avenue
Portland, OR 97209
503-223-1093
www.oblationpapers.com
Ribbon, cards, office supplies, and
decorative paper

Preservation Hall Antiques
7919 S.E. 13th Avenue
Portland, OR 97202
503-238-9912
Antiques, home and garden accessories

Van Dykes Restorers
Catalog request: 800-237-8833
Customer service: 800-787-3355
www.vandykes.com
Antique and reproduction products

Wally's Music Shop
607 Washington Street
Oregon City, OR 97045
503-656-5323
Musical instruments

Waverly
800-423-5881
www.waverly.com
Wallpaper and fabric

Zeldaloo Studios
Owners: Alisa and Mark Timmerman
7853 SE 13th Avenue
Portland, OR 97202
503-235-5675
Info@zeldaloo.com
www.zeldaloo.com
Original art by various artists

Additional thanks to the following women for their beyond-creative assistance:

Kimberly Lewis
503-580-3016
junker4life@yahoo.com
Handmade lamps, including the slip-covered
lampshades featured in Chapter 3

Suzanne Martin
martinhoops@comcast.net
Slipcovers and curtains

Jolene Owens
maggielockwood@comcast.net
Handmade lamps, including the hattie lights
featured in Chapter 3

Amanda Ransier, Owner
Bon Chic
404 NW 10th Avenue, Suite 100
Portland, OR 97209
Furniture and home accessories

It's important to surround myself with women such as yourselves. For additional location shots, thanks to Annelle Friel. And very special thanks to my handyman, Harold Keever, who made many of the projects featured in this book.

Contents

Introduction

Rules, rules, rules. You've heard them throughout your whole life. Color between the lines. Don't wear white after Labor Day. Wait an hour after you eat to go swimming. And when it comes to decorating, there seem to be rules for that, too. Follow the color chart. Always group items in threes or fives. Don't paint your house any color that might make it hard to resell! I mean, really, can you imagine if we listened to all that mumbo jumbo?

I've written this book to celebrate rule-breaking in design—to teach you to listen to your instincts and become confident in developing your own unique decorating style. When it comes to decorating and design, I don't think outside the box—because I never had a box to begin with! I want you to embrace the same attitude.

The same goes for when you're flipping through these pages. This book is not something you will read left to right, start to finish. Each chapter has its own distinct theme, but many of these concepts overlap each other. So don't be surprised if you find yourself skipping back and forth from one chapter to another! Remember, no rules.

In this book you'll discover quick and easy decorating tips that you can incorporate into every room. At the end of each chapter, step-by-step projects will guide you in making some of my favorite creations your own. I've even shared some of my own personal bloopers so you won't make the same mistakes I have. Hey, even designers flub once in a while!

So don't be afraid to take risks, and have fun! Paint up a storm, build keepsakes out of junk, mix old furniture with the new, and remember never to swallow gum because it will stick to your ribs (just kidding!).

If it walks like a duck ...
it must be a flower pot.

1

Recycling Meets Decorating

"**W**hat made you think of that?" If I was given a dime for every time I've been asked that question, my son's college education already would be paid for—and he won't be a freshman until the year 2020. I don't think creativity can be explained in one simple answer; it's a recipe of multiple thoughts. Sounds deep, huh? But not really. All you need is a touch of craziness, a pocketful of mistakes, big gobs of humor, a limitless amount of imagination, and a dive-in-head-first attitude. And hey, if you don't have all the ingredients, that's what I'm here for!

One thing that gets my blood pumping is seeing something used for something other than what its original purpose was. For example, ice tongs as a paper towel holder, or bicycle parts as decorative wall art. That's the fun of decorating: You'll never be punished for trying new ideas, and your home will become an inspirational hot spot for those who need help in the vision department.

Decorating Tip

I'm always dressing things up—literally. Wrap a belt, any belt, around a flowerpot. Or tie the rim of the pot with a bandana, or even a bungee cord.

It's a cinch. We won't say who got too big for his britches.

My son, Chase, is full of the unexpected. So is his room. The origin of the shelf above the bed is still a Quimby mystery.

Make curtain tiebacks come alive by attaching a simple bottle. Heck, if you have floral patterned curtains, you could even match them with the real thing!

Decorating Tip

Napkins make great curtains. Add a little conversation piece by using vintage pot holders as curtain rod finials.

These were nasty 1970s back porch railings. And now—positively elegant window toppings. Best of all: Free is a very good price.

Found in the basement of an old house I used to live in: my fancy, smancy paper towel holder. Note the twine used to hang the holder, and the braided seat cover hiding an outlet on the wall.

Decorating Tip

Always have a supply of sticky tac on hand. It comes in a putty form, and I use it constantly. Here, it holds these little tin coasters in place on the front of my kitchen cabinet.

My friend Annelle's garden umbrella is sewn from chenille bedspreads—some new, some old.

Don't be swayed by convention. Here's a swingin' way to serve high tea. Really high tea.

Decorating Tip

One of the best resources for bedspreads is a seasonal or year-end sale. That's where you really catch a bargain. Slap my hand if I ever pay retail.

We removed the fringe from each of the bedspread panels and attached each strip of fringe to a panel of a different color.

Project

Floor Board Fridge

It wasn't in the budget. When we remodeled the house we couldn't afford the kazillion-dollar refrigerator—the one with the custom-made panels to go with the custom made-cabinetry. So, I bought a cheaper fridge with the capability to have panels, and I made the panels myself. These are my old kitchen floorboards slendered down to slide into the panels of the fridge. The scrap fabric covers the ugly plastique water dispenser. My reward: Nobody notices my fridge. My job is done!

Supply List:

Refrigerator that allows panel
    doors to be inserted (mine is
    a General Electric)

Chop saw

Screwdriver

Scissors

Table saw

Block sander

Measuring tape

Sticky-back Velcro tape,
    ½-inch wide

150-grit sandpaper

11 boards cut to the size of your
    refrigerator doors; ours were
    3¼ x 67 x ¼ inches (We
    used salvaged tongue and
    groove fir floorboards from
    our old kitchen.)

Latex paint

Paintbrush

How To:

1. Our refrigerator was designed to fit ¼-inch-thick panels. Check yours to see what size panels it can accommodate. Then, with the table saw, cut the boards to the correct thickness.

2. Measure the height of the refrigerator doors. With the table saw, cut the boards to the height of the inside of the panel frame.

3. Measure and cut the last 2 outside boards of each door to the correct width. The end boards might overlap the refrigerator door.

4. Sand the bottom edges.

5. Paint the boards.

6. Unscrew the top plate of the refrigerator. The outer side frames will fall off when you remove the top.

7. Attach 6 strips of the fuzzy portion of the Velcro vertically to the refrigerator.

8. Attach the scratchy portion of the Velcro down the length of each board.

9. Working from the center to the outside, assemble the boards one at a time to the refrigerator.

10. Reassemble the outer side frames. They are magnetized.

11. Reattach the top plate. This will hold everything together.

Project

Horseshoe Box

Supply List:

Old wood box

Pair of horseshoes with 2 holes predrilled in each tip (Just about any hardware store will drill the holes for you.)

4 screws
(It doesn't matter if they are flathead or Phillips, but they do need to be larger than the hole that is in the horseshoe and shorter than the width of the box.)

Screwdriver

Sheet of sandpaper (100 grit)
(1 standard sheet will divide into 4 sections that fit snugly on the hand sander.)

Hand sander (optional)

Leftover paint

Cheap paintbrush

How To:

1. Paint your box and then let it dry.

2. Using your hand sander (if you have one) and sandpaper, sand the entire box.

3. Center 1 horseshoe with its points pointing down, and position it about $1\frac{1}{2}$ inches down the outside of the box. You want to have enough room to grip the horseshoe like a handle.

4. Drill the screws in.

5. Repeat on the other side.

It's kick boxing! A pair of apple crates branded with Quimby style.

Project

Kitchen Cabinet Frame

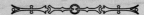

Supply List:

Kitchen cabinet door with all the hardware removed

Tree branches (They need to be fairly straight and long enough to frame the cabinet door.)

Band saw

Screwdriver

8 screws

How To:

1. Using the band saw, cut the branches in half length-wise.

2. Place the flat parts of the branches on the cabinet. Place 1 on each side, and then place the other 2 horizontally on top of the other branches, forming a box.

3. At each corner of the makeshift frame, screw the branches into the cabinet.

A 1920s kitchen cabinet door and yard debris came back to life as a picture frame.

Project

Window Frame Art

Supply List:

Window, preferably without
  the glass
Cardboard pieces large enough
  to cover the window openings
Art that you want to frame
Glue stick
Scissors
Duct tape
2 nail spikes
Hammer
Level

How To:

1. Cut a piece of cardboard to a size slightly larger than the opening of the window frame. The window in this photo is a 3-pane window, but 1 piece of cardboard covers all 3 openings.

2. Cut and paste your art onto the cardboard.

3. Duct tape the cardboard to the back of the window.

4. Hammer 2 nails side by side (use your level if needed) into the wall. This will keep the window from tipping side to side.

5. To mount the window, just poke the nails through the cardboard at the top of the window frame. This is a somewhat primitive way to hang it, but it works for me!

Color Outside the Lines

We have all made the mistake of choosing the wrong color at one time or another. My infamous color faux pas was thinking that the perfect shade of green for the exterior of my house matched an old croquet ball—Kermit the Frog green, to be exact. Well, the house was green, alright! Friends and family said things like, "It's not so bad," or, "I'm kind of getting used to it," or, my favorite response, "It's horrid! What were you thinking?" Ah, the love . . .

Why share this with you? Because if I didn't take the chance, I never would have found the right shade of green that currently adorns my home. Have fun with color. Don't take it so seriously. Mix and match. Live a little, and when you do paint, don't be lazy like me—change out of your good clothes.

> **Who says** the color wheel has to be round?

I'm not stringing you along. These were the inspiration for the color palette for this room.

I had so much fun decorating the living room of my good friend Cindy Cowell. She is such a girlie girl—she doesn't even own a hammer. She thinks nails are something you get manicured.

Decorating Tips

Say It Isn't Sew

1. Replicate this window treatment by draping raw yard goods over a curtain rod for a soft and delicate effect. You don't even need to finish the edges.

2. Tuck a quilt around the seat cushions on your couch.

3. Repeat your colors on both large and small scales. Here, pink walls are balanced by pink flowers and candles.

31

The whole color scheme for this living room was inspired by a piece of cantaloupe and a red-and-brown coffee cup. The walls are the tasty, edible part of the cantaloupe. The floral drapes and seat cushions are the rind. The ottoman, pillows, trunk, and chairs are the coffee cup. When choosing colors, most people take paint chips and fabric swatches with them. Whenever I went shopping for paint, fabric, furnishings, or accessories, I always had a piece of cantaloupe and the coffee cup in hand.

Breakfast at Tiffany's—well, her name is really Lindsey.

Decorating Tip

Once you've chosen your colors, don't second-guess yourself. Don't listen to your mother-in-law. Stay on course.

Color. When people ask me, "How do you put together your colors?" they are looking for a deep answer. My answer is: Head for the produce section of your grocery store. Or swing by the nearest fabric outlet. Check out your child's classroom projects. I've even taken a close-up photograph of the double center line on a busy street to capture just the right yellow.

Finding my muse.

Decorating Tip

Decorating Tip

One of my secrets of color balance is repetition of more than one color.

Something old. Something new. Fresh flowers tucked into 1960s glass grapes. Everybody used to have these.

Seven different shades of blue. Six variations of green. Just about every shade of tan imaginable. And a splash of orange.

Project

Hanging Bike Parts

When using many colors throughout a room, find creative ways to tie in the accessories with the color scheme. Here, spray-painted bicycle parts that match the fabrics of the furniture complete the look.

Supply List:

A variety of sizes of bicycle chain rings and cogs (There are 9 in this photo.)

Satin spray paint (Use different colors.)

Degreaser solution

Ribbon (We used 4 different colors of ribbon, too.)

How To:

1. Remove all the grease from the chain rings and cogs.
2. Spray paint each one on both sides. Let dry.
3. Tie one end of each ribbon to each bike part and the other to the curtain.

Decorating Tip

Bike cogs and rings look great as holiday ornaments, and they create a wonderful sound when used as wind chimes.

Project

Drop Cloth Curtain

Supply List:

*Painter's drop cloth
   (We used a 9 x 12, purchased
   at Home Depot.)*

*7-foot-long wood dowel, $1\frac{1}{2}$
   inches in diameter*

Four $\frac{1}{4}$-inch eyehooks

Four $\frac{1}{4}$-inch S hooks

Electric drill

Drill bit ($\frac{3}{16}$ inch)

Rope, approximately 9 feet long

Scissors

*Two 4-feet-long, $\frac{1}{8}$-inch-wide
   chains (The ceiling here is 11
   feet high, and we hung the
   curtains 4 feet from the ceiling.)
   Make sure the chains can hold
   up to 50 pounds.*

Fabric scraps (optional)

2 clamps

Tape measure

2 dozen upholstery T pins

How To:

1. Clamp the dowel to a table and drill a hole into the dowel 3 inches in from each end.

2. Screw an eyehook into each of the drilled holes.

3. Spread the drop cloth out on the floor, and lay the dowel 5 inches from the top end of the drop cloth. (You can determine which end you want to be the top.) Flip the remaining 5 inches of cloth over the dowel, covering it.

4. Using T pins, fasten the 2 pieces together. Remember, the dowel should be between the layers of fabric.

5. Make small slices through both pieces of fabric about 5 inches apart and 3 inches from the top. Do this all the way across the drop cloth.

6. Tie a knot in one end of the rope, and then weave the rope through the holes to the other end. Tie that end off, too.

7. Measure the inside distance from one eyehook to the other. This will be your guide as to how far apart to measure the holes on the ceiling.

8. Once you've measured, drill your holes in the ceiling and screw an eyehook into each of the drilled holes.

9. Attach an S hook to each ceiling eyehook, and then hook the chain on each end.

10. Attach an S hook on each dangling end, and then attach the dowel to the S hooks. (Optional: To disguise the chain, hide it under wrapped scraps of fabric.)

Decorating Tip

This drop cloth creates a neutral back drop, using the dangling colors to link the wall to the color scheme of the room. To add pizzazz and a bigger splash of color, replace the drop cloth with a floral-patterned king-sized sheet, or drape multicolored twin sheets over the rod.

The great thing about old hats is that they all have stories. Hats such as these have been stored in attics for thirty or forty years. Not only are they beautiful, but they all have a story. So take them out of the attic or off of your head, and put them up in the air. (See project directions on page 52.)

3

Let There Be Light

I never can leave well enough alone. Take lamp-shades, for example. The majority of them are Plain Jane boring. They come in colors of beige, white, off-white, white-beige, or beige-white. Now, there's nothing wrong with that, and if you have a house full of them, I don't have a problem with it. But I'm just saying (one of my husband's favorite lines: "But I'm just saying...") they represent to me a blank slate ready to be altered, enhanced, or tossed out and replaced with something totally different.

Lamp and ceiling medallions, a base from a broken terracotta urn, and an old Christmas tree stand all create beautiful bases for candles.

Yeah, that's me: life of the party.

I don't have a thing to wear to the ball. Sheer, full-skirted prom dresses made a great window treatment.

Quick change. Dress up a shade by tying bandanas around it. Slip in a greeting card. Here, I also added miniatures on a whim. The result? Instant personality.

My friends are the story of my life.
-Helen Keller

I'm not too crazy about lamp cords. I love old sconces, but the downside is that they are usually plug-ins. Disguising yucky cords can be as simple as A-B-C. Here I transformed the entire cord by attaching salvaged stencil forms and clip-on earrings.

Decorating Tip

For a different look, you can substitute clothespins for the earrings I used here to dress the cord. The sky's the limit. You could attach family photos, children's art, or dried flowers. For a modern flair, use black office clips and black-and-white photos.

Project

Slip-Covered Lampshade

Supply List:

Floor lamp (found at local junk shop)

Old shade with no fabric, just wire (bought at a garage sale)

Vintage slip (bought at an auction yard)

2 yards white muslin fabric

1 yard pink cotton fabric

5 tea bags (green tea is what I had in the cupboard)

Sewing scissors

1 bottle of icy white folk art paint

Any old paintbrush

Brown thread

Safety pins

1 yard hand-dyed silk ribbon (found at a boutique, dyed by a local artist)

How To:

1. Make a pot of tea and leave the tea bags in the water.

2. Take the muslin outside and spread it out on the grass, then pour the tea over it, leaving the tea bags on the fabric. This will make the fabric darker in some spots than others. Let it dry in the sun.

3. Paint the base of lamp with the icy white folk art paint.

4. Cut $\frac{1}{4}$ inch into the muslin fabric, then tear two 4-inch strips of the longest length of the fabric.

5. Sew a $\frac{1}{4}$-inch seam along the length of the fabric.

6. Turn the fabric strips right side out, then thread them over the neck of the lamp. The strips should be longer than the neck to get the scrunchy look. Tie them with the hand-dyed ribbon at the top to hold them in place.

7. Put the shade on, then put the slip over the shade (it should hang way too low).

8. Take the safety pins and gather up the sides of the slip so the ruffles are all that hang down. Pin the fabric one section at a time, hooking each pin around a lampshade wire. Do this for every wire around the lampshade—there should be 5 or 6.

9. Cut a $\frac{1}{4}$-inch strip into the pink fabric, and tear off $1\frac{1}{2}$-inch strips (as many as you need to cover the safety pins used).

10. Loop a strip of the pink fabric around each wire, and tie a bow over each safety pin to hide it.

11. Fluff and enjoy! Always be sure to check wiring in old lamps and, if needed, have them professionally rewired. Use proper wattage for the size of your shade, and make sure your slip does not fall through the wires to touch the light bulb.

Remember all the times your mom said, "Wear a slip—I can see through your dress"? She's absolutely right. The "peek-a-boo" transparency of this slip has transformed a B-L-A-H blah lamp shade into a Cinderella lamp. Rags to riches.

Project

Hanging Hattie Lights

Supply List:

Vintage hat (The more flowers it has, the better.)

Silk flowers and crinoline (to fill in the empty spots)

Ribbon

Lace

Buttons

18-gauge wire (optional)

Wire cutters (optional)

Glue gun

Glue sticks

Beads

Fabric

Raffia

Electrical cord (It's best to use the kind with an on/off switch.)

25-watt bulb

Fabric to cover cord (optional)

Safety Features

1. Always be sure to turn the lights off when not in use.
2. Use only a 25-watt bulb.
3. Keep cords out of reach of children.

How To:

1. Select the hat and accessories that you want to use.

2. If the hat has bare spots, apply silk flowers and/or tucked crinoline with your glue gun to hide them.

3. Wrap the electrical cord with ribbon (other wrapping options include strips of fabric, raffia, or fabric cording).

4. With the hat in an upside-down position, sew a button through the ribbon and hat to hold the two together. (If you prefer to sew the ribbons to the hat without using buttons, cover the stitching with small silk flowers.) Repeat two more times; three ribbons just look better. If you choose to use wire to attach the ribbon to the hat, wrap the wire in the ribbon before attaching it.

5. Insert the electrical cord between the ribbons. Tightly tie the cord in place with ribbon or wire. When measuring the length of the cord, keep in mind that you do not want the bulb to touch the inside bottom of the hat.

6. Screw in the light bulb.

Decorating Tip

Also pictured here: I used decorative clothing pins as personal glass markers. These are always winners as housewarming gifts. You also can use them to pin a napkin to a glass.

Project

Feathered Table Lamp

Supply List:

*Table lamp base that has holes where
the original glass shade was attached*

Vintage hat

Scissors

25-watt (or less) light bulb

Needle and thread

How To:

1. Cut a small hole (approximately ½ inch) in the top center of the hat by pinching the hat together and making a little snip.

2. Using a needle and thread, sew the center of the hat to the underside of the rim.

3. Screw in the light bulb.

One of my favorite ways to quickly transform any type of lighting is to use period hats and bonnets. The original shade for this brass lamp was way too modern for my taste. So, I replaced it with this sleek feathered number.

Project

Hattie Light Floor Lamp

Supply List:

Floor lamp

Vintage hat

25-watt light bulb

Screwdriver

Scissors

How To:

1. Cut a small hole (approximately ¼ inch) in the top center of the hat by pinching the hat together and making a little snip.

2. Remove the light socket so that the lamp cord is exposed. Poke the lamp cord through the center hole in the hat.

3. Replace the light socket. It screws in, and this will pinch the fabric between the socket and the lamp.

I was just about ready to leave an estate sale empty-handed when I poked my nose into the hall closet. The ruffled edge of this straw hat guaranteed it a ride home with me. The price: one dollar.

Project

Cardboard Lampshade

Supply List:

Wall sconce
Inexpensive lampshade
Pieces of corrugated cardboard
Glue
Rubber bands
Light bulb

How To:

1. Rip all the straight edges from scraps of the cardboard.
2. Note that you will be attaching the cardboard starting at the bottom of the shade and slowly working your way up and around.
3. Place glue on the smooth side of a cardboard piece and wrap it around the lampshade.
4. Wrap a rubber band around the shade and cardboard to secure the piece in place.
5. Let dry.
6. Repeat the same process with the remaining pieces of cardboard, making sure the pieces overlap each other until the shade is completely covered.

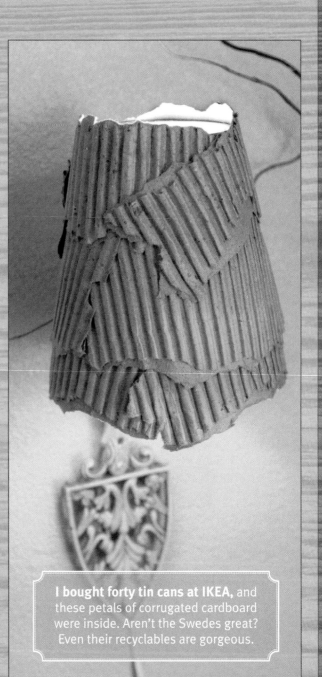

I bought forty tin cans at IKEA, and these petals of corrugated cardboard were inside. Aren't the Swedes great? Even their recyclables are gorgeous.

Wrappin' It Up

Supply List:

Hanging light with a chain

*Fabric strips (This light is covered
   in chenille scraps.)*

Fabric fringe

Scissors

How To:

1. Tie one end of a fabric strip to the ceiling
    medallion and start wrapping the strip
    around the light chain. When the strip
    starts to run out, just tie another strip on.
    Don't tie the strips all together first.
    You'll get all tangled up when trying to
    cover the chain up.

2. Continue the process until the whole
    chain is covered up. Tuck in some fabric
    fringe at the bottom and the top.

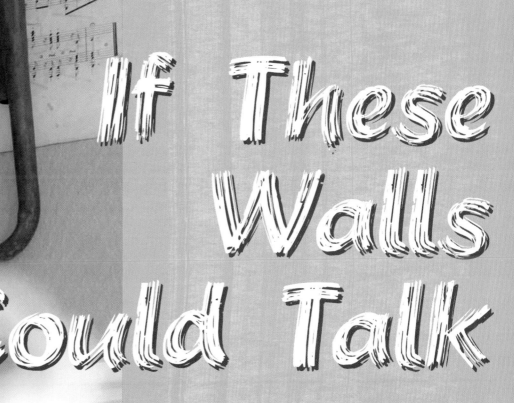

4

If These Walls Could Talk

G ame show survey says: "Nine out of ten homes play it safe by placing on the wall three ____ evenly side by side?" The answer? Frames! Come on—let's have some fun instead! Hang up a downspout and turn it into a planter. Circle a mirror with chicken wire. A bare wall, door, or any flat surface, for that matter, is an open invitation to showcase your decorating personality. Let your walls do the talking. They are a clean canvas waiting for you to display your art, old hardware, musical instruments, cleaning supplies, or even your galoshes.

Thanks for the memories. My Grandma Lillian's sheer lace blouse is displayed with family heirlooms passed down to me. My grandmother would be so happy that her things are noticed on a daily basis instead of stashed in the attic.

Outhouse. This rescued garden trellis is a multi-purpose piece. Decorative and functional, it organizes jewelry—and brings the outside in. Mr. Gnome greets you. Soapstone letters on the door help guests find their way.

BATH

Built entirely with recycled materials by my handyman, Harold Keever, this one-of-a-kind kitchen island is the focal point of the great room. We incorporated a column at one end and a half-column at the other, custom built cupboard doors from recycled exterior house siding, and crowned it all with an old picket fence. I'd drawn the concept on the back of a napkin. So much for detailed plans.

Without losing precious square footage and natural light, these windows hanging from the ceiling allow for the separation of living room and dining room.

Thermostats in the center of the wall are a decorator's nightmare. I understand the purpose of thermostats; I just do not like looking at them. Here's one great solution: chalkboard wall panels.

Decorating Tip

Take this concept one step further and use chicken wire as a seasonal backdrop. Save a tree—hang your ornaments here, instead. Tuck in some autumn leaves to create a swag. Hang decorative Easter eggs (which came first, the chicken wire or the eggs?).

Why did I create a window valance out of chicken wire? Some things you just can't explain.

I found these seashell broaches at Portland's Bon Chic, one of my favorite stomping grounds.

I turned this old medicine bottle into a wall vase. By adding a wonderful worn frame with peeling paint, I created my very own still life.

Project

Hanging the Bugles

Toot your own horn. While driving through Oregon City, Oregon, something in the window of Wally's Music Shop caught my eye. It was a kettle drum filled to overflowing with rusted bugles. I thought it was an awesome window display, but the truth was that the drum and its contents were just minutes away from the dumpster. So, as I usually do, I rolled up my sleeves and started digging. The bugles were dirty and dented, and all were missing some part here or there. I thought: SAH-WEET! Just another day in the life of Shannon.

Supply List:

Musical instrument

Upholstery pins

Salvaged sheet music

Sticky tac

How To:

1. Place a small amount of sticky tac on the backside of each corner of the sheet music.

2. Press the sheet music to the wall.

3. Using upholstery pins, mount the musical instrument on the wall over the sheet music.

Project

Hang Ups

Supply List:

Antique frame without the glass

Colorful sheet of decorative paper
(The paper must be larger than the
inside measurements of the frame.)

Masking tape

Sticky tac putty

Ribbon, approximately 1 yard

Brass or wooden letter

Scissors

Mounting nails

Everyone likes to see their
name in print. This simple project
makes a great conversation piece.

How To:

1. Lay the front side of the frame on the floor.

2. Lay the sheet of paper on top of the back side of the frame, making sure it covers the whole opening.

3. Cut the paper approximately ½ inch wider than the opening.

4. Use the masking tape to attach the paper to the back side of the frame. Pull it tight so it does not sag in the center.

5. Hang the frame up on the wall with a mounting nail.

6. Center your letter inside the frame and nail it to the wall, right on top of the paper.

7. Grab your ribbon and sticky tac putty. Press a small amount of the sticky tac onto one end of the ribbon.

8. Press the ribbon to the back side of one top corner of the frame. Repeat on the other side.

9. Find the center of the ribbon. Place sticky tac on the back side of the ribbon, and press it onto the wall above the frame.

Decorating Tip

Instead of brass or wood letters, use felt.

Project

Vintage Jewelry Board

Supply List:

Vintage frame, preferably oval or round,
   with the glass removed

Large piece of foam core

Fabric (We used velvet.)

Paint

Wide ribbon

Glue gun

Polyester batting

4 small nails

Box of pearlized sewing pins

How To:

1. Paint the frame your desired color.
   We used an antique white here.

2. Cut the foam core to fit onto the back of
   the frame.

3. Cut the fabric and polyester batting to a
   size 3 inches larger than the foam core.

4. Wrap and hot glue the polyester batting
   to the foam core, then repeat this step,
   adding the fabric as the top layer.

5. Insert the wrapped foam core into the
   back of the frame, and attach it with
   4 small nails.

6. Using a hot glue gun, attach the ribbon
   to the back of the top edge of the frame.

7. Hang and enjoy!

Decorating Tips

1. Use pearlized sewing pins to attach jewelry—
   such as earrings, bracelets, and necklaces—
   to the board.

2. You also can create this project to use as a
   memo board or to display old family photos.

3. Feel free to be creative with this project and use
   a fabric that reflects your personal style. Not
   much fabric is needed, so you can use anything
   from a vintage tea towel to a old chenille quilt.

No more tangled jewelry. My friend Amanda created this storage-on-display solution to the jewelry glob.

Project

Supply List:

Sticky-back Velcro (can be purchased at any fabric store)

Tin trays (I used 4 here.)

Scissors

How To:

1. Cut a piece of Velcro to the length of the tray.

2. Peel off one side of the Velcro and press it in the center of the cabinet door.

3. Peel the other side of the Velcro, center the tray over it, and press firmly.

> Leaning against the countertop backsplash are 1950s TV-dinner trays. I paid two bucks for six trays—only fifty cents a tray! Can't beat that. What's great about these trays is that they are storage on display. Extra guests for dinner? No problem. Just take them down and extend your dining space.

Decorating Tips

I like using the sticky-back Velcro because it seems to hold heavier items better, and if your mounted object is crooked, it is easy to correct.

5

Containers, Vases, and Pots— Oh My!

If an object can hold something, it qualifies as a container and/or vase in my book (no pun intended). There are no limitations as to what an object can be used for—whether it's a functional purpose, like growing flowers, or a showcase for your collections. Use your imagination, and a tennis ball retriever becomes a toilet paper holder. Newspaper delivery tubes convert to flower vases, and canning jars remind you to take your vitamins. The great thing about this concept is that you can use anything lying around the house. Take my husband's coffee mug that never makes it into the dishwasher, for instance. Voila! It now holds my hair accessories. Nothing is safe in my house!

It's a tennis ball retriever! With a supply within arm's reach, you'll never hear, "We're out of TP."

Costume jewelry instantly dolls up a colorless vase. Add marbles, and you're good to go.

Decorating Tip

Grandma's old clip-on earrings clamped all around the rim of the vase look great, too.

Dried hydrangeas are so delicate. Displayed above reach in this ice cream bucket, they'll keep forever.

This tin downspout's main purpose was to keep the water out. My purpose is to keep the water in. I inserted a Tupperware container filled with dirt and an indoor plant.

Decorating Tip

Musical instruments can be used as containers anywhere in your home. In the bathroom holding hairbrushes. By the front door collecting outgoing mail. Or anywhere filled with fresh flowers when you insert a small vase inside.

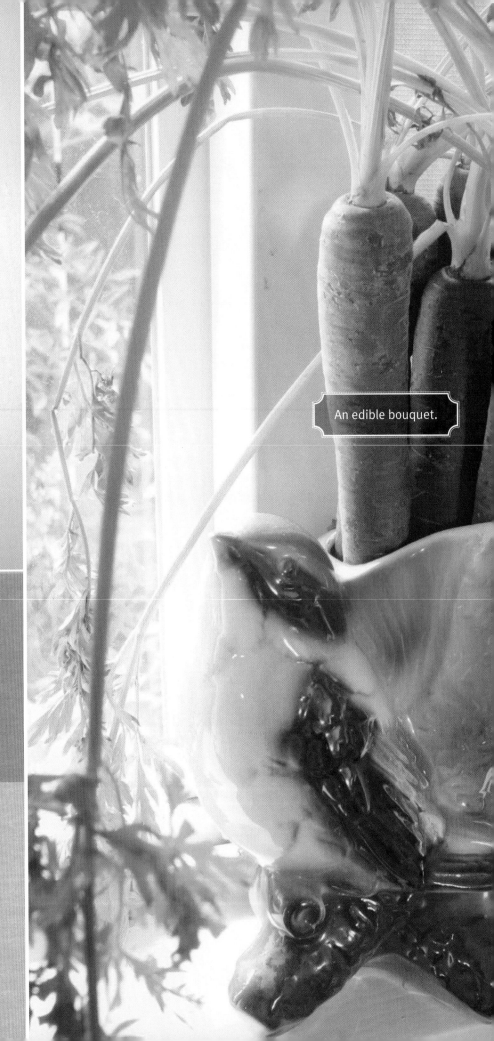

An edible bouquet.

Talk about being on its last leg. The only thing left on this purse is its frame and lining. The fabric is stained and worn. The clasp doesn't close. It's ripped and frayed. But in my eyes it's still beautiful.

As I said earlier, in our home, nothing stays put. Take the red tin garbage can I was using in my office, for instance. Have you ever noticed how garbage cans have gotten larger over the years? I got tired of emptying this adorable but small red bin every day, so I decided to fill it permanently with flowers.

Decorating Tip

If you choose to plant your flowers in these tin garbage cans, do what I do and poke holes in the bottom for drainage. Garbage cans also look great in groups of three hanging side by side used as paper and envelope organizers.

"Mommy, where's my hat? Have you seen my other glove? Wha'cha do with my boots?" In the winter, this is the morning conversation trying to get out the door. Solution: Put them where they can see them—right under their noses. But I guarantee they'll still ask.

Anything to speed up the morning routine. This purse works wonders.

81

Project

Canning Season

I stole this idea from my Grandpa Buzz, who was a part-time carpenter. His very neat and tidy workshop had rows and rows of canning jars nailed under the shelves. They held nuts and bolts, nails and screws, and what Grandpa called whatchamacallits. I brought Grandpa Buzz's storage solution into the kitchen. Same concept—different contents. As you can see, the apple doesn't fall far from the tree.

Supply List:

Canning jars with tin lids

Screwdriver

Screws

Hammer

Nail

How To:

1. Using a hammer and nail, poke a hole in the center of a canning jar lid.

2. Screw the lid into the underside of a shelf. Make sure that your screw is not longer than the width of the shelf wood. Sharp points sticking up from underneath is not a good thing. We used ¼-inch screws here.

3. Tighten jar around lid.

Decorating Tip

Canning jars aren't just for the kitchen. In the bathroom they can organize Q-tips, cotton balls, and vitamins. Elsewhere, they can be used as piggy banks or to store animal treats.

Project

Message in a Bottle

Supply List:

Chair
Ribbon
Bottle
Rubber band
Water
A single flower

How To:

1. Wrap the rubber band around the neck of the bottle.
2. Pull part of the rubber band away from the bottle and thread the ribbon through it.
3. Wrap the ribbon around the bottle to hide the rubber band.
4. Tie the ribbon onto the back of the chair.
5. Add water to the bottle and finish it off with a flower.

Decorating Tip

Write a special message on a piece of paper and insert it into the bottleneck.

Project

Hanging the Newspaper Can

Supply List:

Old metal newspaper can

Spray paint

Screws

Screwdriver

Any water-tight container that will
fit in the newspaper can

How To:

1. Clean the newspaper can.

2. Spray paint the newspaper can with
   any color and sheen that you prefer.
   Used here is a glossy green.

3. Place the water-tight container
   inside the can.

4. Add flowers.

Decorating Tip

*I like old and rusty patina. This can has the
original paint on it. I love displaying history.*

A newspaper can converted into a fabulous flower vase will guarantee friendly conversation. Be sure you have a water-tight container inside. Trust me—I learned the hard way. Notice I'm not showing you the stained carpet below.

6

Trading Places

W hen you stop noticing what's on display in your home, it's time for a change. Become your own "piano mover" and shake things up a bit. A dining room table feels right at home at an outdoor party; a child's cradle stores wooden blocks during the day before being transformed into living room furniture at night. Rearranging your home furnishings is light on the pocketbook, creates instant gratification, and gets feedback such as, "When did you get that piece?" The only slight problem: previous carpet indentation.

The red doll crib that my great-grandfather made sometimes holds my son's blocks near the end of his bed. In other rooms, it is the weekend sports center.

Decorating Tip

Wagons are great for small spaces. For a condo or apartment patio, fill with potted plants to create a garden. Entertaining outside? Stock with beverages or roll out a dessert tray.

In our household, **we are always on the move.** And that includes the furniture. Anything on wheels isn't going to sit still for long. Advance, migrate, or become extinct: If we get tired of a piece in one room, we move it to another.

Pinwheel in pretzels—why not?

The curtain in this room is actually an old bedspread, draped so you would never know that it is ripped and torn and faded.

Project

Window Screen Leaves

> **A moveable feast.** We use this table inside and out. Here we're "leave-ing" it in, decorated with old window screen leaves. See page 125 for patio use.

Supply List:

Window screen (Screen that is aged by the weather works best for this project.)

Scissors (It's fine to use the crusty dull pair that doesn't cut very well.)

Newspaper

A variety of shapes and sizes of leaves

Fabric paint that comes in a tube (I have used Scribbles 3D paint and Jones Tones pearl paint in the past.)

Wood scraps

How To:

1. Cover your table with newspaper.

2. Place your wood scraps and leaves on the newspaper, making sure that they aren't touching one another.

3. Lay the window screen over the leaves and wood scraps. You want to have a little space between the screen and the newspaper.

4. Looking straight down on the leaves, take your paint tube and start outlining the shape of each leaf. Do not touch the tube to the screen because the paint will seep through to the other side.

5. Let the paint dry.

6. Cut around the outer painted edges of each screen leaf. (Hint: Always give the tube of paint a good downward whipping motion before squeezing. This keeps the paint near the top and prevents air bubbles. It's no fun when you are right in the middle of tracing your leaf and—pop— an air bubble splatters your paint.)

Project

Bucket on a Stand

Supply List:

*6 pieces of flat strap metal, each
 approximately 3 feet long
 (You should have some extra
 to work with.)*

Wire feed welder

Heavy leather gloves

*Welding helmet with a 9/10
 shade lens*

Bench vise

Hacksaw

Pencil

Locking Pliers

Galvanized bucket

How To:

1. To form the circular base that will hold the bucket, select a piece of strap metal that is about $1^{1}/_{2}$ times the circumference of the galvanized bucket in length. (This will give you extra metal to hang on to while bending it.) Place one end of strap metal into the bench grip and slowly bend the metal to begin to form a circle. Reposition the strap 1 to 2 inches lower in the vise to continue to bend the metal until it forms a complete circle that is slightly smaller than the circumference of the bucket's rim.

2. Square the ends together and, using the hacksaw, cut one end off so it's not overlapping the other.

3. Weld the ends together.

4. Repeat steps 1–3 to form the smaller strap metal circle that will form the base of the bucket stand. I made mine about half the circumference of the top circle.

5. Select 4 pieces of strap metal that are all the same length. They will become the legs.

6. Lay 1 leg piece of strap metal over the outer portion of the circle and clamp it with the locking pliers.

7. Weld the leg on.

8. Measure 3 other evenly spaced points on the outer rim of the circle so that the legs will be equally set apart.

9. Repeat steps 6 and 7 until all the legs are attached.

10. Weld the smaller circle to the inside of the legs, approximately 3 inches above the ground.

11. Let the metal cool, and then set the bucket into the top.

Bucket on a stand. I can't take credit for this idea. I saw something similar in a very expensive home accessories catalog—for hundreds of dollars. "Well, I can make that," I said, and I did. I find all of my buckets at garage sales, and I never spend more than two dollars—and often get the dented ones for free. In the summer months, see it outside as a portable fridge. In wintertime fill it up with cozy quilts and blankets in the living room.

7

More than Three? A Collector Makes Thee

Clutter: Eye sore or beautiful display piece? I prefer the latter, but I do have to admit I am guilty of the unsightly pile. Isn't that what closets were made for? I choose to display my many collections in an organized manner. I do this for a couple of reasons. One, organization creates more room for more stuff, which gives me the green light to go shopping. Two, organized clutter becomes displayed clutter, which then becomes a showplace for collections. Hey, look at that, my clutter just became a valuable collection! Now that's a glass that's half full!

Hide it in plain sight. Organized and messy can live harmony.

Decorating Tip

Displays of affection. To hold photos vertically, use flower frogs.

Pillow Talk. This stack of pillows is my take on *The Princess and the Pea* (see her jewels hanging from the headboard?). These down-filled pillows feature the original ticking fabric: striped, floral, and ivory. Beauty, plain and simple.

I confess. I'm a shoebox album type of gal, so this is my happy medium: Display half-finished photo albums with loose photos on top of them. It's a constant reminder— in a pretty way—to get the job done.

This collection adds up to more than the sum of its parts. Flash cards pinned to the curtain overlay make homework fun!

Pin ups. When displaying the different shapes and sizes of your collection, think of a class photo. Tall in back, short in front.

An abundance of like objects can be beautiful. Buttons are full of memories. It's a shame to have them stored in a jar hidden in the closet. And have you ever noticed that you never throw away a button? Trust me, you are a button collector. Have you checked your junk drawer lately?

Short stack. Provide more elbow room by stacking your cake stands. At breakfast, fruit and pancakes can be offered together.

Having a ball. Instead of a flower bed in this shady backyard garden, we rolled out a border of balls. You'll never have to water them.

That's me, all wrapped up in my work.

Project

Doorknob Candlesticks

My workshop is full of extra hardware. This is one clever way to repurpose those castaway doorknobs you've been collecting. Filled with slender beeswax candles, the brass and porcelain surfaces glow and reflect light.

Supply List:

Vintage doorknobs (Select knobs that have a flat surface, so each knob stands still while in the upside-down position.)

Thin candles

How To:

1. Remove any hardware from the door-knob. Don't forget that tiny screw that might be inside of the knob.

2. Turn the doorknob upside down, making sure it lays flat.

3. Insert the candle into the doorknob.

4. Optional: Place the doorknobs among pebbles and rocks to help prevent them from tipping over.

Decorating Tip

Instead of pebbles, use rice, popcorn, beans, or florist marbles underneath the doorknobs.

Project

An outside room can be defined by a collection of 1940s and '50s tablecloths. To create a nostalgic feel, choose the ones that still have the berry stains on them from summertime jelly jams. They'll look like the national flags of American home-cooked meals.

Supply List:

Outdoor trellis
Vintage 1940s and '50s tablecloths
Clothespins

How To:

1. To create this walk-through wall, grab a corner end of a tablecloth and use clothespins to clip it to the top inside corner of the trellis.

2. Repeat this process all the way across the trellis to the other side.

Decorating Tip

If you don't have a trellis in your yard, tie a rope from tree to tree, or drive two stakes into the ground and connect a rope to them, creating a clothesline.

Project

Rock Slides

Supply List:

Rocks of various sizes that have smooth surfaces to write on

Permanent marker

Clear shellac sealer and finish

¼-inch paintbrush

Gloves

Sticky tac putty

How To:

1. Clean your rocks with soap and water. Let them dry completely.

2. Write a word on each rock.

3. Seal the rocks with the shellac. The sealant gives the rocks a nice shine and makes them smooth to the touch. Let dry.

4. Stack the rocks randomly up against a kitchen counter backsplash.

5. Optional: Use sticky tac to secure the rocks to one another.

Decorating Tip

Put these in potted plants. Use them as paperweights. Even give them as thank-you cards. You also can stack rocks along a bathroom backsplash or highboy dresser backboard.

When I remodeled a girlfriend's kitchen I asked for a list of her favorite words. No explanation. My housewarming gift was a randomly placed backsplash of inscribed rocks.

8

Create Your Own Style

How many times have you walked into a friend's home and discovered something in the decor that you've never noticed before? Follow that lead and be daring. Put a drinking fountain in your mud room, paint words or phrases in unexpected places, decorate your table with outrageous objects. If someone asks why, respond: Why not?

Yes, I am a member of the "don't tell anybody, but I love gnomes" club.

Bunny found a new home—
hopping out of the garden and
into the family room.

Honey, wha'dja do with my boots?
They're where you left them!

Decorating is an expression of yourself, not an intimidating book of rules. This quaint living room is filled with recyclable accessories. The couch is actually a 1950s hide-a-bed slip-covered with chenille bedspreads and linen tablecloths. The yellow wooden daffodil on the wall used to be a garden stake. And who would ever think that a Victorian floral armchair could be paired with retro tropical print pillows?

This placement gives the phrase "bird's-eye view" a whole new meaning.

If the shoe fits... These one-inch-tall leather boots belonged to a lost doll.

The mirror broke, but the frame lives on. Its original wood backing makes for a perfect bulletin board.

Doing the dishes is one of my least favorite chores. So, I put a drinking fountain in the house.

This adorable fluff head was a cake decoration. How could I have packed him away after the party?

Remember all that tissue paper you save—then can't find when you need it? Frame it. On the back of the frame write a note with the location of the stored tissue.

Project

Supply List:

Masking tape

Scissors

Ball of string

Knife

Various shapes and sizes of vases

Cheerios

Fruit, such as oranges, limes, lemons,
cherries, bananas, apples

Cut flowers

How To:

1. Cut a piece of string to a length of 2 feet.

2. Tie a knot on one end.

3. Wrap a piece of masking tape around the other end to create a makeshift needle, making it easier to thread the Cheerios.

4. Thread Cheerios the full length of the string.

5. Tie a knot at the other end.

6. Cut the fruit up in wedges.

7. Place the fruit wedges around some of the vase rims.

8. Fill the vases with flowers and fruit.

9. Weave Cheerios strands around the vases.

My inspiration for this idea was a Froot Loop necklace that my preschooler made for me. Do you know the life expectancy of boxed cereal? I don't—but my necklace still looks great after nine months.

Project

Ready. Aim. Fire.

Supply List:

Carbon paper (You can find this at a craft store.)

Interior latex semi-gloss paint

Artist's paintbrush

Computer

Copy machine

Masking tape

8 x10 white paper

Pencil

Clear shellac sealer and finish

4-inch throw-away paintbrush

Gloves

How To:

1. Using a word processing program, type the word you wish to create in your choice of font, and print it out.
2. Enlarge the word to the size you want.
3. Tape the sheet of carbon paper ink-side-down on the floor.
4. Tape the piece of paper containing the word on top of the carbon paper.
5. Trace the outline of each letter.
6. Carefully lift both pieces of paper off the floor.
7. Paint the word the color of your choice.
8. Seal the word with the shellac sealer and finish. This will give the surface an aged look. Let dry.

Safety Tip

When working with shellac, keep away from heat, sparks, and flame. Use only with adequate ventilation. Avoid prolonged breathing of vapor or extended skin contact.

Here is an old photo of the students at an all-male boarding school in which there is one woman among the 250 men. I put up stencils spelling the word "DISCOVER" and hung a magnifying glass to create my own version of "Where's Waldo?"

In my household I am out-numbered four-to-one in the gender department. I never miss. I painted the word "AIM" in front of the toilet.

Project

Hanging Bike

Supply List:

18-gauge wire
Small bicycle
3 maps
1 screw
Sticky tac
Screwdriver
Wire cutters

How To:

1. Place a small amount of sticky tac on each corner of each map and press them up on the wall.
2. Wrap the wire around each handle bar.
3. Secure screw in the wall.
4. Hang the bike up.

No wonder he's smiling. This covered patio is bursting with color. The exterior wall is deep purple. Throw in some primary red, sea blue, and apple green in all textures and sheens, and it balances itself.

Too cute to part with. Chase's first bike displayed like the trophy it is—no more training wheels.

Project

Braided Drawer Pulls

> **Self Expression.** With good intentions my Grandma Lillian was going to make a rug out of these braided rag balls. That was more than sixty years ago. That project never got done, but on a smaller scale, it became braided drawer pulls on my dresser.

Supply List:

Scissors

An assortment of scrap fabric

Any type of drawer with 2 holes in it

How To:

1. Gather a variety of patterns and colors of fabric. I like to combine 3 to 6 different fabrics for one braid.

2. Rip or cut each strip of fabric to a width of about 1 inch. Before tying the strips together, poke them all through one of the holes in your dresser drawer and then tie them in a knot from the inside of the drawer. You might need to make the hole slightly larger than it currently is to fit them through.

3. Pull the rags taut so that the knot clogs the hole and prevents the fabric from coming undone. Begin braiding. It doesn't matter if the lengths differ; when you start braiding the strips together and one becomes shorter, just tie on another strip and continue with the same process until you reach your desired length. The finished braid should be at least long enough to grab onto without touching the drawer.

4. Poke the other end of fabric inside the drawer and then tie a knot. Cut off any dangling strips.

Decorating Tips

1. Rag handles also look great on kitchen cupboards. As long as they have two holes it will work.

2. Replace your tassel tiebacks with your braided ropes to create a fun and whimsical environment.

3. Ordinary wire baskets look complete when a braided handle is added.

From Drab to Fab books, by the editors of *Country Sampler Decorating Ideas*, show you inexpensive, easy ways to revitalize your home using color and personal touches.

Starting with the basics, both books introduce you to the materials and techniques you'll use to transform your furniture, your walls, and your home. Each chapter covers a different style or technique, and then presents four separate step-by-step projects complete with color photos of every part of the process, including before-and-after photos.

Furniture Fix-Ups: 75 Easy Ideas for Fresh New Looks shows you how to save money and have fun revitalizing old furniture and flea-market finds. You'll be introduced to techniques ranging from decoupage to stains and dyes, painted patterns to transferred images. You'll learn to create a crackled paint look, use punched tin to give a cabinet new life, and use stenciling to add interest to an old armoire, plus lots of other inspiring projects!

Paperback $19.99
ISBN: 1-57860-225-4

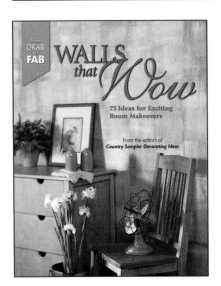

Walls That Wow: 75 Ideas for Exciting Room Makeovers shows you how to give your home a completely new look with the least expensive, easiest home decorating tool available: paint. By taking a chance on innovative color and creative painting techniques, you'll learn quick, easy methods for washes, textures, stencils and stamps, murals, patterns, and much more.

Paperback $19.99
ISBN: 1-57860-224-6

The From Drab to Fab books are available at local booksellers as well as online at www.emmisbooks.com